I'M A CHEF

Contents

BEFORE YOU START

1 All measurements are in cups and spoons. These are level measurements. Level off the contents of the cups and spoons with a knife.

2 Always wash your hands first.

3 Wear an apron to stay clean.

4 Check your ingredients and utensils and get them out before you start cooking.

5 Use oven mitts when handling hot plates and dishes. Ask an adult for help when using an oven.

6 Be careful with knives.

7 This symbol means, "Ask an adult to help you."

GUACAMOLE

Guacamole is a dip, usually eaten with corn chips. In Mexico, it is eaten spread on tortillas before or with a meal, or as a side salad.

YOU NEED:

2 ripe avocados

1/2 teaspoon lemon juice

1 tomato

1/2 onion

dash of Tabasco sauce

2 tablespoons chopped cilantro or parsley

1

Cut avocados in half. Remove pit.

5

Peel and finely chop onion. Add to bowl with dash of Tabasco.

2

Scoop out avocado.
Put into bowl.

3

Add lemon juice.
Mash well with a fork.

4

Chop tomato. Add.

6

Add cilantro.
Mix well with a fork.

7

Put pit into
guacamole. This will
help keep guacamole
from turning brown.

8

Serve with tortilla chips
or as a side salad.

CHICKEN TERIYAKI AND RICE

Chicken and rice are eaten around the world. In Japan, soy sauce, ginger, and sesame give this dish its distinctive flavor.

YOU NEED:

1/2 cup soy sauce

1 teaspoon grated root ginger

3 tablespoons sugar

3 tablespoons sesame seeds

4 pieces of chicken (leg or breast)

1 cup long grain rice

1 teaspoon salt

water

 Set the oven to 375°.

1

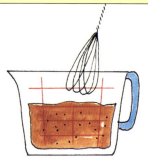

Put soy sauce, ginger, sugar, sesame seeds in bowl. Stir.

5

Bring a big pan of water to a boil.

2

Put chicken in a baking dish.

3

Pour sauce over chicken. Bake for 45 minutes.

4

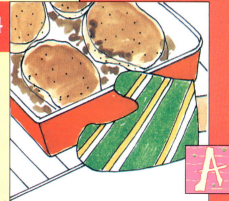

Every 15 minutes, brush sauce over chicken.

6

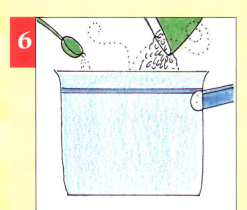

Add rice and salt.

7

Boil rice, uncovered, for 10 minutes. Stir occasionally.

8

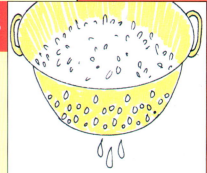

Drain in colander. Serve with chicken.

HAMBURGERS

Hamburger was originally called "hamburg steak." It was named after Hamburg, Germany. Here's how to make your very own hamburgers at home!

YOU NEED:

2 cups lean ground beef

1 teaspoon salt

4 hamburger buns

garnish options: ketchup, mayonnaise, mustard, lettuce, tomato, onion, cheese

1

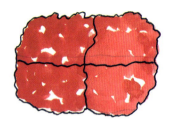

Divide beef into 4 equal amounts.

5

Place meat patty on bottom half of bun.

2

Roll into balls, then press out into flat circles.

3

 Lightly salt a skillet. Fry patties in skillet until browned.

4

Put patties on paper towels to soak up any extra fat.

6

Garnish with lettuce, tomato, onion, and cheese.

7

Spread top half of bun with mayonnaise, mustard, or ketchup.

8

Put two halves together. Serve.

POTATO SOUP

Potato soup is a favorite in Ireland and many northern climates. Because of their high starch content, corn, potatoes, and squash are the base for most hearty soups.

YOU NEED:

4 large potatoes

1 onion

2 tablespoons butter

3 cups water

2 teaspoons instant chicken stock powder, or 1 cube bouillon

1 teaspoon salt

a dash of pepper

1/2 cup milk

1/2 cup grated cheese

2 tablespoons chopped fresh parsley

1

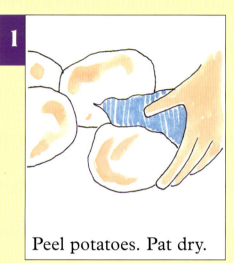

Peel potatoes. Pat dry.

5

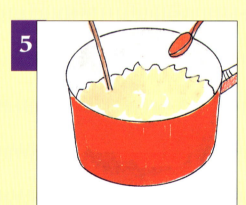

Add water, stock powder, salt, pepper. Stir.

2

Grate them coarsely.

3

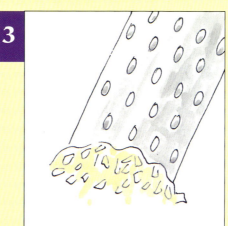

Peel onion. Grate it.

4

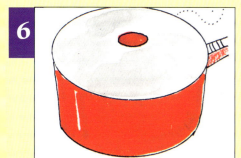

Put butter, onion, and potatoes in a big pan. Turn on stove to high.

6

Bring to a boil. Turn to low. Cover. Simmer for 20 minutes.

7

Add milk. Stir well.

8

Ladle into bowls. Sprinkle cheese and parsley on top.

CLUB SANDWICHES

Sandwiches are named after the Earl of Sandwich, who ordered a servant to bring him two slices of bread with a piece of roast meat between them.

YOU NEED:

BLT Club:
mayonnaise
cooked bacon
3 pieces of toast
lettuce
tomato

Veggie Club:
mayonnaise
3 pieces of bread
tomato
lettuce
cucumber
sprouts

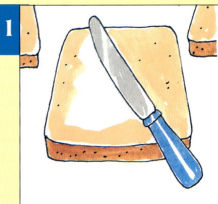

1

Spread mayonnaise on 3 slices of toast.

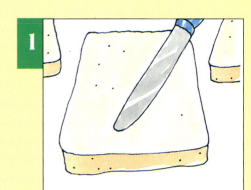

1

Spread mayonnaise on 3 slices of bread.

2

Layer first slice with bacon. Top with the second slice of toast.

3

Layer second slice of toast with lettuce and tomato.

4

Top with third piece of toast. Cut sandwich in quarters.

2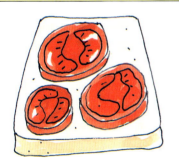

Layer first slice with tomato. Top with the second slice of bread.

3

Layer second slice of bread with lettuce, cucumber, and sprouts.

4

Top with third piece of bread. Cut sandwich in quarters.

SHORTBREAD

In earlier times, shortbread was often stamped with designs before baking. Shortbread from Scotland is famous throughout the world.

YOU NEED:

1 1/2 cup flour

1/2 cup powdered sugar

1 cup soft butter

Set the oven to 375°.

1

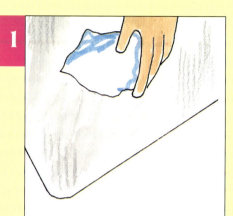

Lightly grease cookie sheet.

5

On floured surface, roll each ball out into an 18 cm circle.

2

Sift flour and mix with sugar in a bowl. Cut butter into small cubes.

3

Mix butter into flour and sugar until it sticks.

4

Knead mixture lightly. Divide it into 2 balls of dough.

6

Pinch edges with thumb and index finger. Lightly mark in triangles.

7

Put circles onto a cookie sheet. Bake about 20 minutes, until golden.

8

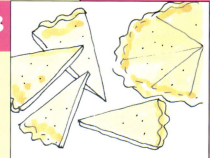

Cool on tray. Sprinkle with a little sugar. Break into wedges.

BUTTER COOKIES

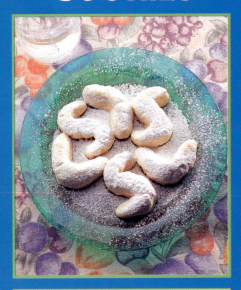

In Greece, these cookies are called Kourabiethes. At Christmas, these cookies are often topped with cloves to symbolize the Three Wise Men.

YOU NEED:

1 cup butter

1/2 cup sugar

1 egg

2 1/2 cups all-purpose flour

1 teaspoon baking powder

1/2 teaspoon vanilla extract

1/2 teaspoon almond extract

about 2 tablespoons powdered sugar for sprinkling

 Set the oven to 375°.

1

Beat butter, sugar, and egg until smooth.

5

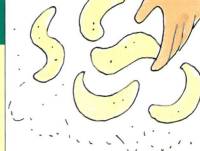

On a floured surface, shape into crescents or S-shapes.

2

Sift in flour and baking powder. Mix well.

3

Add vanilla and almond extract. Mix well.

4

Form teaspoonful clumps of dough into balls.

6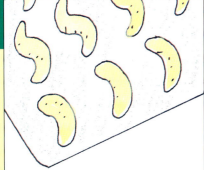

Place 5 cm apart on cookie sheets.

7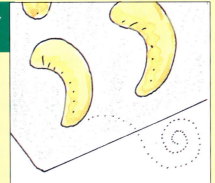

Bake 15 minutes or until golden on edges.

8

Cool on wire rack. Sprinkle powdered sugar over cookies.

LAMINGTONS

Lamingtons first appeared in recipe books after World War I. They are named after Baron Lamington, the governor of Queensland, Australia (1897 to 1901).

YOU NEED:

1 store-bought sponge cake about 20 cm x 20 cm

4 cups powdered sugar

1/4 cup unsweetened cocoa powder

1 tablespoon melted butter

1/2 cup milk

3 cups shredded coconut

1

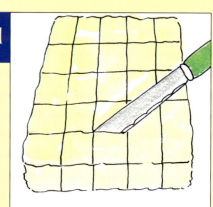

Cut cake into squares about 5 cm x 5 cm.

5

Add melted butter and milk.

2

Put hot water 5 cm deep in a pan.

3

Sift powdered sugar and cocoa into a heat-proof bowl.

4

Put the bowl into the pan of water.

6

Stir well until smooth.

7

Using 2 forks, hold a square of cake. Dip it in icing until covered.

8

Toss cake in coconut. Let icing set – about 1/2 hour.

MINI PAVLOVAS

Named after a famous ballerina, Pavlovas are a white, light meringue dessert. Decorate with New Zealand kiwi fruit and other fresh fruit.

YOU NEED:

2 egg whites
(at room temperature)

1 cup powdered sugar

1/2 teaspoon vanilla extract

1 teaspoon cornstarch

1 teaspoon vinegar

4 tablespoons boiling water

whipped cream and sliced fresh fruit for decorating

 Set the oven to 300°.

1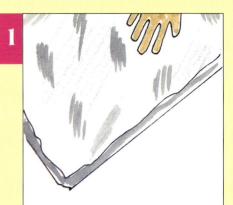

Line a cookie sheet with foil. Grease foil.

5

Beat fast for 15 minutes.

2

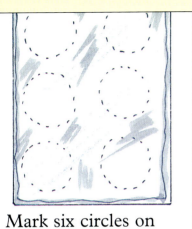

Mark six circles on foil.

3

Put egg whites in a bowl. Beat with an electric mixer until mixture is stiff.

4

Add sugar, vanilla, vinegar, cornstarch, and boiling water.

6

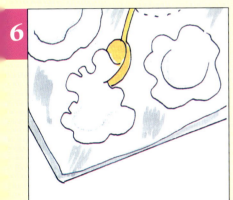

Spread mixture on each circle, shaping into nests.

7

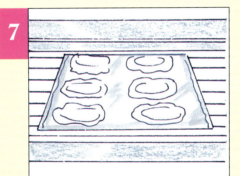

Bake 15 minutes. Turn oven off. Leave in oven until cool.

8

Peel off foil. Put on plates. Spread with whipped cream and decorate with fruit.

SWEET TREATS

This sweet treat is a popular recipe from Brazil and is a favorite at children's parties.

YOU NEED:

2 cups sweetened condensed milk

1 egg yolk

1 tablespoon butter

1/2 cup shredded coconut or ground nuts

1

Put condensed milk in pan. Add egg yolk.

5

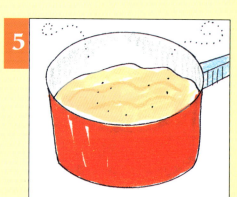

Take off heat. Cool about 1 1/2 hours.

2

Over low heat, stir constantly for about 25 minutes until mixture thickens.

3

Use a spatula to stir and scrape sides of pan.

4

Stir in butter.

6

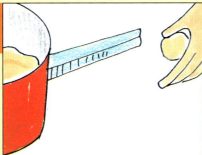

With wet hands (to prevent sticking) roll mixture into small balls.

7

Roll each ball in coconut or ground nuts.

8

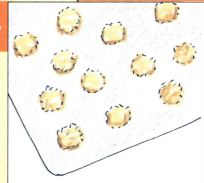

Put on tray. Store in a cool place until set.

COOKING DICTIONARY

Add Put in.

Bake Cook in the oven.

Beat Mix very fast with a spoon or beater.

Bring to a boil Cook liquid until it bubbles.

Chop Cut in small pieces.

Drain Pour off liquid.

Extract Concentrated flavor of a plant, nut, or seed.

Floured Cover a surface with thin layer of flour to prevent sticking.

Form Mold ingredients into a certain shape.

Fry Cook in hot oil or butter.

Garnish Add decorative or tasty things to food.

Grate Cut by scraping off little pieces with a grater.

Grease Make a surface slippery by applying oil or butter.

Knead Fold dough toward you, then push it away.

Ladle Scoop out liquids with a large dipping spoon.

Line Cover a pan or tray with foil or waxed paper.

Mark Indicate lines by making little indentations in dough.

Mash Soften and break apart with a spoon or fork.

Melt Heat a solid until it becomes a liquid.

Mix well Stir all ingredients until they are blended together.

Peel Remove the outer peel or skin of a fruit or vegetable.

Pinch A small amount.

Roll Flatten out dough with the help of a rolling pin.

Sift Mix together dry ingredients.

Simmer Cook over low heat until liquid is hot, but not bubbling.

Spread Cover a surface with a sauce or cream, usually using a knife or spatula.

Sprinkle Scatter over food.

Stiff Condition of egg whites beaten until they form peaks and hold shape.

Stir Mix with a motion going around the bowl, pot, or pan.